Simple & Simply Delicious

I am very fortunate to have the most wonderful family and the most caring friends that anyone could every wish for. Thank you for always being there for me.

To my husband who has always believed in me, and who supports me in all my endeavors, I love you dearly and enjoy every moment of this great adventure we share.

Introduction

Family, Friends & Food

Food has always been an important part of my life. In the French culture we spend a lot of time at the table. We find it difficult to separate food from life, because it is during those special moments as we share a meal that we discuss life.

We always look forward to the next gathering of friends and family, the next meal, the next opportunity to share with the people we care so deeply about. *S'est la vie.*

Food therefore for us is not just about the meal that we consume but the personal connection that we experience with the people at the table with us. It is the reason why we may spend hours at lunch or dinner eating, talking, and enjoying life.

Spending hours at the table eating however does not mean that you need to spend hours in the kitchen preparing the meal. It is possible to have a wonderful 4-course meal after spending only minutes in the kitchen preparing it.

In France, a meal may start with an aperitif, which is small drink to excite your appetite. This could include a *champagne, kir royal, pastis* (a French alcohol)*, pinot de Charentes* (cooked wine) or other drinks depending on the region of France that you are in. Different kinds of nuts or 'finger food' can be served with your drink.

After an aperitif you may have a starter. Depending on the time of year, this could be a salad, soup, a quiche or something light to start your meal with.

You will notice no rush between courses at a French table. A meal is to be enjoyed, and every course should be a pleasure.

The main course would then follow with *Boeuf Bourguignon, Cassoulet, Canard a l'orange* or possibly a local specialty like *Lentils and Sausage.*

After which will be a cheese platter followed by dessert, coffee and a *digestif* (a strong alcohol such as Cognac, Calvados or Armagnac).

Simple & Simply Delicious teaches you how to prepare these wonderful meals and much more. In addition to French delicacies I've also included recipes from a variety of exotic countries. You will learn how to create these meals using everyday ingredients found in your local supermarket.

After you have learned how to create these meals you can present them *a la carte* (individually) or *le menu* (as multi-course meals). Menus are presented towards the end of the book that shows you how to use these recipes to present 3 or 4 course meals. From this you can prepare a feast. Best of all, you can do this with spending only minutes in the kitchen.

France

The city in France that I am from is called *Le Puy-en-Velay*. It is in the *Auvergne* region in France, which is in the center of the country. It is one of the most beautiful regions in France, surrounded by forest and countryside. The region offers some of France's most delicious meals. Among other things, *Auvergne* is knows for its famous green lentils, its cheese and its *charcuterie* (sausage, hams, pate etc.).

Le Puy-en-Velay is a historic city, dating back to the original Pilgrimage. It is a traveler's paradise and includes artifacts and historical monuments including: *the Notre-Dame cathedral, the Black Virgin, the Rocher Corneille with the Notre-Dame-de-France statue, and the Saint-John baptistery.*

Notre-Dame-de-France statue, Le Puy-en-Velay

Polignac, France

International Food

      I left France some years ago and have traveled to and lived in a good portion of the world. In each country I have enjoyed experiencing and learning the culture, the history and the delicious local flavors of that country.   With each trip, the opportunity to try local spices, herbs, and share recipes have been a pleasure.

      Each country has its own flavor with food. I love traveling and when I visit a country I always eat the way the locals do. There is good food to be found in France, Spain, Italy, Greece, Jamaica, Cuba, Egypt and practically anywhere else you may travel to. Throughout the book, I will share some experiences with you regarding local foods that I experienced in my quest for adventure and my search for great meals.

Spice market, Cairo Egypt

Sphinx, Giza pyramid Egypt

8

Dingle, Ireland

Lake Tahoe, CA

Simple & Simply Delicious Meals

As I travel I've found that there are certain meals that I could prepare in any country that I traveled to because they use basic ingredients that could be found in any supermarket anywhere in the world. These are tried and true recipes that I've prepared and enjoyed over the years and that I use when I get together with my friends or family anywhere I visit. They are also the meals that I share with new friends as I travel. These recipes use a mixture of common herbs such as thyme, parsley, bay leaves, and basil and also spices such as curry, ginger, cinnamon, saffron and chili peppers. This along with meats and vegetables that create exotic meals that one could only imagine finding in some far away land. The meals are simple to prepare, and are extremely delicious. In other words, meals that are simple and simply delicious.

These simple and simply delicious recipes are very practical to prepare and can be used for romantic dinners, family get-togethers, parties and a variety of other events. It is a great opportunity to share with others in your life. It's the best gift one could ask for. In fact, someone might enjoy receiving this book as a gift as well.

In this book you will find a collection of recipes that I have learned from my home in France and from my travels throughout Europe, Asia, the Middle East, North America and the Caribbean. The flavors are absolutely delicious and I hope you enjoy sharing a simple but simply delicious meal with someone close to you.

Table of Content

Starters

11

Moule Mariniere   49
Bruschetta   50
Tacos   52
Shrimp and Crab Croissant   43

Main Courses

Couscous   57
Boeuf Bourguignon   58
Black Pepper Filet Mignon   60
Beef Curry   61
Lentils and Sausages   62
Steak With Blue Cheese Sauce   64
Honey and Garlic Pork Chop   65
Marsala Veal Scaloppini   66
Cassoulet   68
Chicken Bouchee a la Reine   69
Fricassee Chicken   70
Jamaican Curried Chicken   72
Turkey Leg in Mustard Sauce   73
Szechuan Chicken   74
Arros Con Pollo   76
Rabbit in a Mustard Sauce   77
Canard a l'orange   78
Duck with pears and raisins   80
Caramelised Quails   81

Curried shrimp   82
Saffron salmon   84
Grilled Garlic Lobster   85
Scallop With a White Wine Sauce   86
Mussels in a Beer Sauce   88
Salmon Pasta Gratin   89
Spicy Red Snapper   90

Cheese Platter

Desserts

Dressings & Sauces

Le Menu

Starters

Exotic Cantaloupe

Ingredients:
Serves 4

2 cantaloupe
½ green pepper sliced
½ red pepper sliced
¼ cucumber sliced
1 cup of big shrimp cooked
2 cup thick yogurt
1/4 cup of heavy cream
½ tbsp Tabasco
2 tbsp chive chopped
Salt and pepper to taste

Preparation: 15 min

1. Cut the cantaloupe and clean it.
2. Slice the pepper and cucumber and with a little spoon make little balls with the cantaloupe
3. In a small bowl mix the yogurt with the heavy cream add the chive chopped, Tabasco, salt and pepper to taste.
4. Pour the mixture in each half cantaloupe
5. Decorate with the shrimp and some pepper on top

Italian Salad

This salad is delicious! The unusual mix of cantaloupe and proscuitto is fantastic. You can serve this salad with grilled meat, such as chicken or pork.

Ingredients:
Serves 6

8 oz penne pasta (1 package)
1 small cantaloupe
2 tomatoes
½ cup fresh basil
½ cup feta cheese (dried tomato, basil or natural feta)
4 slice of Serrano ham (proscuitto)
12 black olives (optional)
1 tbsp lemon juice
6 tbsp. olive oil
1 garlic, crushed
Salt and pepper to taste

Preparation: 15 minutes

1. Cook the pasta in boiling water for 8 to 10 minutes
2. In a medium bowl mix the lemon juice, olive oil and the garlic. Add salt and pepper to taste. Add the basil, chopped finely.
3. Clean, peel and cut the cantaloupe into small cubes.
4. Slice the tomatoes.
5. Slice the Serrano ham and roll each slice.
6. Drain the pasta when cooked, and then place it in the bowl.
7. Add the cantaloupe, tomatoes, the feta cheese crumble, the Serrano ham, and the olives.

Exotic Chicken Salad

This mix of curry with chicken, grape and pineapple is succulent.

Ingredients
Serves 4

1 cup chicken baked and cut up
½ cup green grapes (seedless)
1 cup celery
6 cherry tomatoes
1 ½ tbsp mayonnaise
2 tbsp curry powder
1 tbsp soy sauce
1 lettuce European style (spring mix)
½ pineapple cut into chunks
1 cup mandarin oranges

Preparation: 10 minutes

1. In a medium bowl combine chicken, grapes, celery and the cherry tomatoes.

2. Mix the mayonnaise, curry and soy sauce.
3. Add the mayonnaise mixture to the chicken.
4. Let rest for 2 hours.
5. Add lettuce, the pineapple chunks, and mandarin oranges at the time of serving.

Tips: Sprinkle cayenne pepper on top to add taste and color

Salad Nicoise

Traditional salad from the south of France (Nice). It has become so famous that you can find it anywhere in France.

Ingredients:
Serves 4

1 lb potatoes
1 lb French cut green beans
1 cucumber sliced
3 tomatoes
1 small onion chopped
Onions
1 garlic chopped
4 hard boiled eggs
1 can (6 oz) of tuna in water
10 black olives

Preparation: 20 min

1. Cook potatoes in boiling water for 20 minutes and cut them into small cubes.
2. Boil eggs for 10 minutes.
3. Steam the French beans for 5 to 10 minutes.
4. Sliced the tomatoes and cucumber.
5. Chop the onions and garlic.
6. Drain the tuna.
7. Slice the black olives.
8. Mix all ingredients in a medium bowl.

Tips: Serve with vinaigrette dressing (see recipe on page 140).

Spicy Shrimp Salad

Ingredients:
Serves 4

1 clove of garlic, chopped
¼ onion, chopped
16 jumbo shrimp
Pepper sauce to taste
1 lettuce Spring mix
(European style)
1 tomato sliced
1 small red bell pepper
1 small yellow bell pepper
Salt and pepper to taste

Preparation: 15 minutes

1. In a skillet, cook the garlic and onion until soft.
2. Add shrimp and the hot sauce, salt and pepper to taste.
3. Cook for 5-7 minutes over medium heat.
4. Place the lettuce in a medium sized bowl, then add sliced tomato and sliced red and yellow peppers. Place the shrimp on top.
5. Add salt and pepper to taste.

Tip: You can also add fresh chili pepper to enhance the flavor.

Goat Cheese Salad

Ingredients:
Serves: 4

2 tsp olive oil
1/2 tbsp of thyme
1/2 tbsp of rosemary
½ tbsp of basil
Black pepper to taste
8 slices of soft-type goat
cheese (if to soft to cut put
it in the freezer for few
minutes)
1 cup bread crumbs
2 head Boston lettuce, torn
1 cup cherry tomatoes
1 medium yellow
pepper(s), sliced

Preparation: 10 minutes

1. Cut the goat cheese into slices.
2. Place the olive oil into a deep plate with ¼ tbsp thyme, ¼ tbsp rosemary, ¼ tbsp basil and black pepper.
3. In another plate place the breadcrumbs with ¼ tbsp thyme, ¼ tbsp rosemary, ¼ tbsp basil and black pepper.
4. Coat cheese with the olive oil first and then with crumb mixture and bake in the oven for 10-15 min at 375 F
5. While goat cheese is baking, in a large bowl toss lettuce, peppers and tomatoes with vinaigrette (recipe page 139).
6. Divide salad among 4 plates and arrange goat cheese on top. Serve immediately.

Tuna Apple Salad

Ingredients:
Serves 4

1 can tuna
3 cups torn lettuce
1 apple
1 boiled egg
1 stalk celery chopped
1 cup sliced olives
¼ cup cheese cut in
Cubes
Salt and pepper to taste

Preparation: 10 min

1. Drain tuna.
2. Tear lettuce into bite-sized pieces.
3. Core apple and cut into slices
4. Boil an egg (place egg in boiling water for 8 min) and let it cool under cold water.
5. In a large bowl place the lettuce, tuna, apple, celery, chopped, olives, egg slices and cheese.
6. Salt and pepper to taste

Tip: Serve this salad with whole-wheat bread or crackers. It's also great for sandwiches

Red Bean and Tuna Salad

Ingredients:
Serves 4

2 cup red beans
4 eggs
12 cherry tomatoes
1 onion
1 can tuna
1 can corn
2 tbsp thyme
1 cup chicken broth
Salt and pepper

Preparation: 15 min

1. Soak the red beans for 6 hours (or overnight).
2. Pour the beans and the soaking water into a big pot (add some water if needed, the bean should be covered with water). Add the broth, the thyme and 2 pinches of salt.
3. Cook for about 1 hour.
4. When the beans are cooked, drain them and rinse with cold water.
5. Pour the beans into a medium bowl
6. Add the chopped onion, cherry tomatoes, tuna, corn and eggs.
7. Add vinaigrette dressing (see page 140) and serve.

Greek Salad

Bring a touch of the Mediterranean cuisine to your plate with this Greek salad.

Ingredients:
Serves 4

1 pack of Romaine lettuce
1 can pitted black or green olives
1 red onion, finely chopped
1 green and red bell pepper, chopped
2 large tomatoes, chopped, or cherry tomatoes
1 cucumber, sliced
1 cup crumbled feta cheese
Pepper to taste

Preparation: 10 min

1. In a medium bowl, combine the Romaine lettuce, olives, onion, red and green bell peppers, tomatoes, cucumber, and cheese.
2. Salt and pepper to taste
3. You can serve this salad with vinaigrette dressing.

Tip: serve this salad with a Greek dressing see recipe page 141.

Tabbouleh

A traditional Middle-Eastern salad, usually wrapped in lettuce leaves and eaten with the hands. Tabbouleh can also be served with grilled meat or poultry – a perfect summer meal.

Ingredients:
Serves: 4

1 cup fine bulgur wheat
1 lemon juice
1/2 cup olive oil or to taste
2 garlic cloves, crushed
3 medium tomatoes cut in small cubes
1 cucumber cut in small cubes
1 small red pepper cut in small cubes
2 bunches Italian parsley
1/2 cup of garden mint
Salt and pepper to taste

Preparation: 20min

1. Pour 2 cups boiling water over the bulgur wheat. Cover, and let stand about 20 minutes until wheat is tender and water is absorbed.
2. Mix lemon, olive oil, and garlic and pour over the bulgur.
3. Add the tomatoes, cucumber, red pepper, parsley, and mint.
4. Salt and pepper to taste.

Tips. Over the years I've seen different type of tabbouleh. One uses a lot of mint and little bulgur, while the other uses more bulgur and less mint. It depends on your taste. If you prefer extra mint, 2 cups of mint and ½ cup of bulgur

Chinese Hot and Sour Soup

Ingredients:
Serves 6

2 Chicken stock diluted in
5 cups of boiled water
1 tbsp garlic
1 tbsp red Chile paste
5 shitake mushrooms, cut
into thin slices
1/2 tsp. white pepper
4 ounces ground pork
½ cup soy sauce
1 block of tofu, cut into
long strips
½ cup white vinegar
1 ½ cups bamboo shoots
2 tbsp cornstarch
Dissolved in 4 tbsp. water
3 eggs beaten
1/2 tsp sesame oil

Preparation: 20-25 min

1. In a large saucepan bring stock to a simmer. Add the garlic, Chile paste, mushrooms, white pepper, pork, and soy sauce and cook for 20-25 minutes.
2. Add tofu, vinegar, and bamboo shoots. Cook for another 5 minutes.
3. Add cornstarch (previously mixes with 4 tbsp of water).
4. Add the beaten eggs very slowly.
5. Add the sesame oil and stir.
6. Cook another 2 minutes.

Onion Soup

Onion soup originated with King Louis XV of France. He returned home late one night, and all he had to eat was onions, butter, and champagne. He mixed them together, cooked it and had the first French onion soup.[1]

Ingredients:
Serves 4

7 tbsp butter
2 onions thinly sliced
3 tbsp all purpose flour
1 cup beef stock diluted in
1 cup of hot water
2 cups white wine
Salt and pepper to taste
Grated gruyere cheese
French bread sliced and
toasted in the oven

Preparation: 15 min
Cooking: 30 minutes

1. In a saucepan melt the butter and add the onions, stirring constantly.
2. Cook for 6-8 minutes, until the onion becomes soft and brown. Sprinkle flour on top of the onion, stirring at all times.
3. Add 1 cup of beef stock and 2 cups of white wine. Stir until the mixture thickens.
4. Add salt and pepper to taste and bring to a boil.
5. Cover and simmer for 30 minutes to an hour.
6. Serve in soup bowls topped with a slice of toasted French bread and cover with grated Gruyere cheese.
7. Put the soup bowls in the oven to broil until the cheese turns brown on top.

[1] http://www.foodreference.com/html/fonionsoup.html

Greek Vegetable Soup

Ingredients:
Serves 6

2 leeks
4 carrots
1 celery stalks
1 onion
1 garlic clove
1 cup parsley finely
chopped
5 tomatoes cut in cubes
1 can French green beans
1 tbsp. tomato paste
1 tbsp. cayenne pepper
Salt and pepper to taste

Preparation: 20 min
Cooking: 30 min

1. Peel, clean, and slice the leek, carrots, celery, and tomato.
2. Chop the onion, garlic, and parsley.
3. In a large pot add leeks, carrots, celery, onion, garlic, parsley, tomato, green beans, tomato paste, and cayenne pepper. Add salt and pepper to taste.
4. Cover the vegetables with water and cook until boiling.
5. Reduce the heat and cook another 30 min.

Seafood Soup

Ingredients:
Serves 6

1 tbsp olive oil
2 cloves garlic
1 onion
2 potatoes
2 carrots
10 oz shrimp
12 oz red snapper
12 oz kingfish
1 tbsp parsley
1 bay leaf
1 tbsp curry powder
Dash saffron
2 cups white wine
1 ½ cups water

Preparation: 30 min

1. In a large pot, cook the garlic and onions with 1 tbsp of olive oil.
2. Add sliced potatoes, carrots, and water.
3. Add peeled shrimp and cook slightly.
4. Add fish (red snapper and kingfish), parsley, bay leaf, curry powder, and saffron.
5. Cook for 30 minutes.
6. Add wine and cook another 5 minutes.

Tip: You can also use, scallops, cod, or even clams.

Brazilian Black Bean Soup

Ingredient:
Serves 6

2 cups black beans
3 1/2 cups chicken stock
1 cup chopped onion
1 carrot
1/2 celery stalk
6 chopped garlic cloves
3 tbsp cumin
2 peeled, sectioned, deseeded oranges
1/2 cup orange juice
Juice from 1 lemon
1 tbsp red pepper
Salt and pepper to taste

Preparation: 15 min
Cooking: 2 hours

1. Put the beans in a medium pot, cover, and soak them for at least 4 hours (you can also soak them overnight).
2. Drain beans and add the chicken stock.
3. Add salt and pepper. Bring to a boil and then simmer, covered, for 1-½ hours.
4. In a skillet add the carrots, celery, onions, garlic, and cumin. Cook until vegetables are soft. Add them to the beans.
5. Cook for another 15 minutes.
6. Add the orange, the orange juice, lemon juice, and the red peppers.
7. Cook for another 12 minutes.

> **Tips:** This soup is delicious topped with cheese and sour cream.

Cream Of Broccoli

Ingredients:

Serves 4

1 cup water
1 cup broccoli
1 potato cut in small pieces
2 tbsp butter
1 onion, chopped
1 cloves of garlic, chopped
2 cups chicken broth
Salt and pepper to taste
½ cup whipped cream

Preparation: 15 min
Cooking: 20 min

1. Boil the water in a saucepan.
2. Add the broccoli and potatoes.
3. Cook for about 10 minutes at low to medium heat.
4. Melt butter in a different saucepan, then add the onion and garlic and cook for about 3 minutes.
5. Add this to the broccoli, potatoes, and water, and the chicken broth.
6. Puree the broccoli mixture in an electric blender.
7. Pour into a saucepan.
8. Add salt and pepper to taste.
9. Boil the soup and then add the cream.

Country Pie

Ingredients:
Serves 6-8

2 lbs mushroom
½ tbsp cooking oil
4 medium potatoes
5 oz bacon
One short crust pastry
5 oz grated cheese
5 oz sour cream
3 egg yolks
Salt and pepper to taste

Preparation: 15 min
Cooking: 40 min

1. Clean and cut the mushrooms into thin slices. Sauté in ½ tbsp of oil for about 7 minutes.
2. Clean and grate the potatoes. Rinse, then cook in salted boiling water (enough water to cover the potatoes)
3. Cut the bacon and cook it for about 10 min with half spoon of oil.
4. Cover a pie plate with greaseproof paper, then add the first short crust pastry (you will have to separate the short crust pastry into 2 sections).
5. In a bowl mix the mushrooms, potatoes, bacon, and the grated cheese.
6. In a different bowl, mix the cream with the 2 egg yolks (Beat with a fork to mix well), add salt, and pepper.
7. Add the stuffing to the pan top it with the cream and cover with the second puff pastry.
8. Brush the top of the pastry with egg yolk. Make a little hole in the middle of the pastry for the steam, then bake for 40 min at 350 F.

Salmon Pie

This recipe is amazing! Your guest will be very impressed.

Ingredients:
Serves 6-8

1 shallot
1 tablespoon olive oil
½ lb. fresh salmon fillets
3 tbsp breadcrumbs
4 eggs + 1 egg
Fresh parsley, chopped
2 puff pastries
1 lemon
4 big spoon of crème fraîche or sour cream
Salt and pepper to taste

Preparation: 20 minutes
Cooking: 35-45 minutes

1. Chopped the shallot and sauté them with 1 tbsp. olive oil until it become soft.
2. Steam the salmon for about 8 minutes. Remove the skin and bones, and then crumble the salmon.
3. Mix the breadcrumbs, the 4 eggs, the shallot, salmon, and chopped parsley in a bowl. Add salt and pepper to taste.
4. Cover a pie plate with greaseproof paper, and then add the first puff pastry.
5. Pour the stuffing into the pastry and cover with the second puff pastry.
6. Take the yolk of one egg and brush the top of the pastry. Make a little hole in the middle of the pastry for the steam.
7. Pre-heat the oven to 350 degrees and bake the puff for 35-45 min.
8. Add 4 big spoonfuls of crème fraiche to a pan with a little bit of lemon (the quantity depends on your taste).
9. Cut the top of the puff with a knife, pour the crème fraiche on top of the stuffing, and then replace the top of the puff.
10. Bake for another 15 minutes.

Quiche Lorraine

The word quiche comes from the German word "Kuchen," which means, "cake." Vincent de la Chapelle, the chef of Stanislas, King of the Lorraine, made a few changes to the original recipe by changing the bread pastry to a puff pastry. Its new flavor became very popular all over France and is still a favorite traditional dish.

Ingredients:
Serves 6-8

1 tbsp. Butter
5 slices Of bacon chopped
5 sliced of ham chopped
1 onion, chopped
1 clove of garlic
1/2 lb. fresh mushrooms, sliced
9 inch unbaked pie shell
1 ½ cups grated Gruyere cheese or any other grated cheese
3 eggs, beaten
1 cup milk
1 cup cream
Dash salt, pepper
Dash nutmeg

Preparation: 20 min
Cooking: 45 min

1. In a pan sauté the bacon, ham, onion, garlic and mushrooms in butter. Drain on paper towels.
2. Sprinkle this mixture into the pastry shell and sprinkle with half of the grated Gruyere.
3. Beat the eggs in a bowl, and then add milk, cream, salt, pepper, and nutmeg.
4. Pour mixture into pastry shell.
5. Sprinkle the rest of the grated Gruyere onto the mixture and bake for 45 minutes at 350 degrees F.
6. Let the quiche cool for 5 to 10 min before cutting.

Olives Cake

This is an easy recipe, best when served cold. You can cut the cake in small cubes and serve it for an *"aperitif"* with tomatoes or salad and mayonnaise

---

Ingredients:
Serves 6-8

½ cup oil
1 cup grated cheese
(parmesan, gruyere….)
½ cup white wine
4 eggs
2 cup of ham cut in squares
2 cup of green and black
seedless olives
1 cup of flour
1 tbsp of baking powder
Salt and pepper to taste

Preparation: 15 min
Cooking: 45 min

1. In a medium bowl mix the wine, oil and eggs. Add the flour and baking powder.
2. Add the ham, olives and grated cheese
3. Salt and Pepper to taste
4. Bake in a greased 9 in loaf pan for 30-45 min at 375 F

Mushroom Pie

Ingredients:
Serves 3

12 oz of mushrooms
Salt, pepper to taste
1 clove of garlic
1 tbsp dried thyme
¾ cup sour cream
2 egg yolks
1 pinch of cumin
1 puff pastry
2 slices of ham
1 teaspoon spoon of olive oil

Preparation: 20 minutes
Cooking: 20-30 minutes

1. Clean and cut the mushrooms and sauté them with salt, pepper, garlic and the thyme. Cook for about 4-5 minutes.
2. In a small bowl, mix the sour cream, 1 egg yolk, salt and pepper to taste, and a pinch of cumin. Add this to the mushroom and let cool.
3. Cut the puff pastry into 4 rectangles. Place half a slice of ham on each puff and pour a bit of stuffing on one half side of the pastry, then fold the other half side over the stuffing. Press the sides to stick together. Brush the top of the puff with 1 egg yolk so it takes on a golden color.
4. Bake for 20 to 30 minutes at 350 F.

Tips: Serve with lettuce and tomatoes; it's a perfect summer meal

Crab Cake

Crab cakes have become one of the most famous appetizers in the world. There are many ways to cook crab cakes, but here's a delicious recipe.

Ingredients:
Serves 6

1 small onion, finely chopped
½ cup finely minced celery
1 garlic clove
1 large egg
1/4 cup sour cream
1 tbsp. mustard
1/4 cup fresh parsley, chopped
2 tbsp Worcestershire sauce
1 tbsp. red hot pepper sauce
1 ½ cups bread crumbs
1 tbsp olive oil
Salt and pepper to taste
2 lbs of crabmeat

Preparation: 20 min
Cooking: 20 min

1. In a pan over medium heat, saute onion, celery, and garlic in 1 tbsp. oil until soft. Let it cool.
2. Mix eggs and sour cream in a bowl, and then add mustard, parsley, Worcestershire sauce, red hot pepper sauce, breadcrumbs, salt and pepper. Mix well and add to the onion, celery and garlic.
3. Then fold in the crabmeat and shape into cakes. Cook in 1 tbsp. olive oil in a frying pan over medium heat until each side is brown.

Tips: Serve with a salad and a chilled sauvignon blanc white wine.

Chicken Liver Pate

Pate is a French delicacy of finely minced liver, meat or fowl.

Ingredients:
Serves 6

5oz butter
1 small onion, finely chopped
1 garlic clove, crushed
1/2 lb. chicken livers
¼ lb. fresh mushrooms, sliced
2 tbsp Fresh parsley, chopped
1 tsp. Brandy
Dash of pepper
Salt to taste

Preparation: 15 min
Cooking: 15 min

1. Melt the butter in a frying pan add the onion and garlic, sauté until soft. Add the chicken liver, mushrooms, fresh parsley, brandy, salt and pepper, and cook for about 10 to 15 minutes at medium heat (until the livers are brown).
2. In an electric blender, puree the chicken liver mixture. Poor it into a bowl and refrigerate overnight.

Tip: Serve on warm toast!

Prawn Pate

Excellent recipe! It can be served as a snack or as a starter. You can also use salmon or crab instead of prawn

Ingredients:
Serves 6

4 oz butter
1 clove garlic, peeled and chopped
¼ onion, chopped
6 oz peeled prawns
4 tbsp double cream
0.5 tbsp very finely chopped parsley
Salt and pepper to taste
Cayenne pepper to taste

Preparation: 10 min
Cooking: 15 min

1. Melt the butter in a frying pan and sauté onions and garlic until soft.
2. Add the prawns and cook for 5 minutes at medium heat.
3. Puree the prawn mixture in an electric blender.
4. Add the cream, parsley, salt and pepper, and cayenne pepper, and then blend again.
5. Transfer to individual dishes and refrigerate for few hours.

Tips: the amount of the cayenne pepper you add will define how spicy this pate is. Don't add too much!

Moules Marinieres

"Moules Marinieres" are considered the national Belgium dish. Moules marinieres mussels cooked in white wine with butter, shallots, onions and herbs.

Ingredients:
Serves 4

2 oz butter
1 medium onion, chopped fine
4 cloves garlic, chopped fine
2 shallots, minced
2 glasses dry white wine
4 pounds of fresh mussels (buy them already clean)
2 tbsp spring fresh thyme
1/4 bunch parsley, chopped
Salt and pepper

Preparation: 15 min
Cooking: 10 min

1. Melt butter in a large saucepan, and then add onion, garlic, and shallots. Cook 1 minute, stirring at all time.
2. Add white wine, salt and pepper, and the mussels. Cover and simmer 6-8 minutes until shells open, stirring occasionally.
3. Arrange mussels in shells, open side up, on soup plates.
4. Sprinkle with fresh parsley
5. To make the sauce more creamy, 2 tablespoon of cream.

> Tips: Serve with French fries and a chilled Riesling or Chablis white wine.

Bruschetta

"Bruschetta, bruschetta con pomodori" is toasted bread on which you can serve anything you want, such as a vegetable (zucchini, mushrooms, eggplant) and cheese (parmesan, mozzarella or goat cheese). I prefer Bruschetta topped with tomato, basil and garlic.

Ingredients:
Serves 4

12 slices of French or Italian bread
2 clove garlic
4 tbsp. virgin olive oil
2 tomatoes
1/4 onion
1 teaspoon dried or fresh basil
Salt and pepper to taste
5 tbsp of grated Parmesan or goat cheese

Preparation: 15 min
Cooking: 10 min

1. Preheat the broiler.
2. Arrange slices of bread on a baking sheet and broil until lightly browned.
3. In a small bowl, combine 1 garlic clove, and 3 tbsp of olive oil. Brush the mixture on one side of the bread slices.
4. In a skillet, heat the remaining oil over medium heat, then add the tomatoes sliced, garlic, and onion chopped in little cubes
5. Add salt and pepper and the fresh basil. Cook for few minutes.
6. Top the toast with the tomatoes and sprinkle with Parmesan or goat cheese.

Tips: Keep the toast warm until time to serve

Tacos

Tacos can be served on the side or as an entrée

Ingredients:
Serves 6

½ lb. ground beef
½ onion, chopped
1 garlic, chopped
½ cup tomatoes, chopped
½ cup salsa
1 tbsp. chili powder
1 package taco shells
½ cup shredded cheddar cheese
1/2 cup black olives (optional)
½ cup sour cream
2 cups Shredded lettuce

Preparation: 20 min
Cooking: 30 min

1. In a skillet, cook the beef, onion, garlic, and tomato for about 20 min to medium heat.
2. Add salsa and chili powder
3. Fill the shells with meat (half of the shell) and place them on greased paper.
4. Bake shells for about 10 min at 375 F
5. Sprinkle the shells with cheese and put them back in the oven for 2 minutes.
6. Add the olives, sour cream, and lettuce.

Tips: Serve with a Zinfandel red wine or Shiraz.

Shrimp & Crab Croissant

Ingredients:
Serves 4

4 croissants
½ cup sour cream
½ cup of small shrimp
½ cup of crab meat
1 dash nutmeg
3 drop of Tabasco
 Salt and pepper to taste
 1 tsp Dijon mustard
½ cup grated cheese
(parmesan)

Preparation: 20 min
Cooking: 15 min

1. Slice the croissant in half.
2. In a small bowl mix the sour cream with the mustard, nutmeg, Tabasco and salt and pepper
3. Filled on half of each croissant with the mixture.
4. Add the shrimp and the crab
5. Sprinkle Parmesan and cover with the other half croissant

Tips: Serve with a lettuce and a glass of chardonnay

Main Course

Couscous

Several years ago I was traveling to Tunisia with a friend. At the entrance to the desert (Tozeur), we met a young man who would be our guide for the day. He was great and had many wonderful stories to tell us. In the evening he invited us for dinner at his family home, where we met the entire family from grandmother to cousins, and they prepared the best meal I've had .His grandmother shared this recipe with me. We all sat on the ground and enjoy a delightful meal.

Ingredients:
Serves 6-8

1 onion, chopped
5 cloves of garlic, peeled and chopped
4 tbsp olive oil
2 lb chicken thigh or leg
1 lb lamb, cut in cubes
1/4 tbsp cayenne
harissa sauce to taste or pepper sauce.
1 small can tomato paste
3 medium zucchini
4 small yellow squash
3 large carrots
1 can of chickpeas
1 red or green bell pepper
2 ½ cups couscous grains

Preparation: 35 minutes
Cooking: 1 hour 15 minutes

1. In a skillet cook the onion and garlic in olive oil over medium-low heat until soft.
2. Add all spices (cayenne, salt and pepper, harissa) and cook for a few more minutes, stirring as needed.
3. Add the chicken and lamb and cook until brown
4. Add tomato paste, stir for 2 minutes.
5. Clean and cut the vegetables (zucchini, yellow squash, carrots, green pepper, chickpeas) in large chunks and place them in a medium saucepan, add water to cover.
6. Bring to a boil; reduce heat, then cover and let cook for an hour.
7. Pour boiling water over couscous and wait about 5-8 minutes. Fluff with a fork.
8. Place the couscous on a large serving plate and pour the vegetable, chicken, and lamb stew over it.

Beef Bourguignon

Inspired by the cuisine of the French province Burgundy, this savory beef stew can be served with tiny new potatoes cooked in their jackets, or with pasta.

Ingredients:
Serves 6

1/2 cup brandy
2 1/2 cup red wine
4 branches thyme
2 garlic cloves, chopped
1/2 onion, chopped
2 carrots, sliced
4 bay leaves
Salt and pepper
3 lb stew beef, cubed
2 tbsp olive oil
1 tbsp. tomato paste
1/4 cup flour
1/2 lb mushrooms, whole

Preparation: 20 min
Cooking: 2-3 hours

1. Marinate the beef overnight in 1/4 cup of brandy and 1 ½ cup red wine, garlic, onions, carrots, thyme, bay leaves. Add salt and pepper to taste.
2. Pour the flour into a small bowl. Separate the beef from the marinade and coat the beef cubes with this mixture (keep the marinade – we will use it later).
3. In a large pot heat 2 tbsp of oil, then add the meat and brown well on all sides.
4. Add the marinade and the rest of the wine and brandy and the tomato paste.
5. Cover and cook for about 2 ½ hours on low.
6. Uncover and add the mushrooms. Cook for another 30 minutes.

Tips: The longer you cook this dish; the better it gets, but always cooks on low heat. Serve with red wine – a burgundy or merlot.

Black Pepper Filet Mignon

Ingredients:

Serves 4

4 filet mignon steaks
3 tbsp crushed peppercorns
1 tbsp butter
4 tbsp brandy
1 tbsp Dijon mustard
4 tbsp heavy whipped
Cream
Salt to taste

Preparation: 25 min
Cooking: 30 min

1. Start by brushing each filet mignon with crushed peppercorns on each side.
2. Melt the butter in a saucepan and then cook the filets for 6 to 8 minutes, depending on how you like them cooked.
3. Add the brandy and carefully flambé the steaks until there are no more flames.
4. Take of the saucepan from the heat and add cream and mustard
5. Mix well and serve.

Beef Curry

Ingredients:
Serves 6

3 oz grated coconut
8 oz milk
2 lbs beef
2 tbsp olive oil
2 garlic cloves chopped
1 onion, chopped
2 carrots sliced
2 tbsp curry
1 tbsp cumin
1 pinch black pepper
1 pinch coriander
Salt and pepper to taste

Preparation: 35 min
Cooking: 1 hour

1. Boil the milk and add the grated coconut. Cover and let cool for 30 minutes, and then filter the mix. (Through a cheesecloth)
2. In a medium skillet cut the meat in pieces and cook for 10 min with 2-tbsp of oil, the garlic and onions over medium heat.
3. Add the carrots, curry, cumin, pepper, and coriander.
4. Add salt and pepper to taste
5. Add the milk and cook for 1 hour over medium heat.

Tips: serve with basmati rice.

Lentils and Sausages

This recipe is a typical dish from the region where I'm from, le Puy-en-velay (France). We have many way of cooking lentils but here's one of the recipes.

Ingredients:
Serves 4

8 oz lentils
4 Italian sausages (hot or mild).
4 oz of beef polska kielbasa
1 carrot, sliced
1 onion, chopped
1 shallot, chopped
Fresh parsley for decoration
Salt and pepper to taste

Preparation: 10 min
Cooking: 45 min

1. Add ¾ cup water to a pot and boil.
2. Add 1 tbsp of salt, and then add the lentils.
3. Cook for ½ hour at medium heat and drain. (The lentils should be soft)
4. Cook the Italian sausage and beef polska kielbasa in a skillet with the onion, shallot, and carrot for about 30 minutes over low to medium heat. Then add the lentils and cook together for another 7 minutes.
5. Add Salt and pepper to taste
6. Decorate the plate with parsley.

Tips: Serve with Beaujolais or a merlot.

Steak With Blue Cheese Sauce

If you're a blue cheese lover, this is a recipe for you.

Ingredients:
Serves 4

1 cloves of garlic, crushed
5 oz mushrooms
1.7 oz Roquefort or Danish blue cheese
4 steaks
2 tbsp. sour cream
Salt and pepper to taste

Preparation: 15 min
Cooking: 10 min

1. In a skillet cook, the garlic with the mushrooms for 5 minutes.
2. Add sour cream and the Roquefort after mashing the cheese with a fork.
3. Add salt and pepper to taste.
4. Cook for 5 minutes
5. Cook the steak with salt and pepper to your taste. Cooking time depends on how well done you like your steak)

Tips: Serve with red wine Burgundy or merlot.

Honey And Garlic Pork Chop

Ingredients:

Serves 4

4 pork chops
Honey and garlic marinade
(see page 144)
1 onion chopped
1 shallot chopped
2 tbsp oil
Salt and pepper to taste
5 Portobello mushroom

Preparation: 15 min + 2-3 hour for marinade
Cooking: 40 min

1. In a medium bowl mix the honey and garlic marinade, onion, shallot and salt and pepper to taste.
2. Marinade the pork chop for 2 to 3 hours.
3. In a skillet, heat 2 tbsp oil and cook the pork chop (without the marinade) for about 15-20 minutes at medium heat.
4. Add the marinade and the mushrooms to the skillet
5. Cook for another 20 minutes at low to medium heat.

Marsala Veal Scaloppini

This is a typical Italian dish made of veal and a mushroom sauce

Ingredients:
Serves 4

Sauce:
4 garlic cloves, minced
1/2 cup Portobello mushrooms, finely sliced
1 cup small mushrooms
1 cup white wine
½ cup heavy cream
1 tsp. fresh thyme
Salt and pepper to taste

Veal:
Marinade
3 tbsp olive oil
1 tbsp lemon juice
Salt and pepper
2 tbsp fresh thyme
2 tbsp fresh parsley

4 Veal Scaloppini, thinly sliced
Salt and pepper to taste
2 tbsp. olive oil
2 tbsp. unsalted butter

Preparation: 10 min + 2 hours for marinade
Cooking: 30 min

Marinade
1. Mix the olive oil, lemon juice, salt and pepper, thyme, and parsley. Pour over veal and marinate for 2 hours.

The sauce
2. Place the oil in a pan over medium high heat; add the garlic and mushrooms, stirring so the garlic doesn't burn.
3. Add the white wine, cream and thyme. Stir and cook for about 10-15 minutes at low heat. Add salt and pepper to taste.

Prepare Veal Scaloppini
4. Season the veal with salt and pepper and cook with 2 tbsp. butter at medium heat for 20-30 minutes.
5. Add the sauce and cook another 5 minutes.

Tips: Serve with a nice chilled white chardonnay.

Cassoulet

Cassoulet originated in the Languedoc region in the southwest of France. It is made of dried and soaked haricot beans, various pork products (sausage, salted pork), duck, and garlic. This dish is cooked slowly in an ovenproof casserole and topped with a crunchy crust of breadcrumbs.

Ingredients:
Serves 6

1 ½ lb white beans
2 slices of salted pork
2 onions chopped
1 carrot sliced
4 cloves of garlic, crushed
1 thyme branch
1 bay leaf
4 tbsp tomato puree
3 tomatoes
4 large duck breasts
2 sausages
4 oz ham
Salt and pepper to taste
3 oz breadcrumbs

Preparation: 30 min
Cooking: 1 hour

1. Put the white beans in a large bowl, cover with cold water, and soak overnight. Do the same for the salted pork in a different bowl.
2. The next day, drain the beans, cover with fresh water, and bring to a boil. Cook for about 15 minutes. Drain the beans.
3. Cut the pork into large pieces and saute in a frying pan until browned.
4. Put the beans in a saucepan with the onion, carrot, garlic, thyme, bay leaf, and the tomato puree. Cook for 15 minutes.
5. Add 2 tbsp. olive oil to a skillet, and then saute the duck breasts, sausages, and ham cut in small pieces.
6. Put tomatoes in boiling water for about 40 seconds. Peel them and cut in small pieces.
7. Add everything together in a large ovenproof dish and sprinkle the top with breadcrumbs.
8. Bake for about 1 hour at 350 F.

Chicken Bouchee A La Reine

Ingredients:
Serves 4

2 chicken fillets
1 onion chopped
4 garlic cloves chopped
6 oz sliced mushrooms, sliced
1 cup heavy cream
1 red pepper sliced
1 orange pepper sliced
1 yolk
Salt and pepper to taste
4 puff shells
Rice (white or Spanish rice)

Preparation: 30 min
Cooking: 35 min

1. Place the chicken in boiled water for 10 minutes. Drain the chicken and cut into little pieces.
2. In a deep skillet, add chopped onion, garlic, sliced mushrooms, red and orange peppers, and salt and pepper to taste. Cook for about 20 minutes over medium heat.
3. Mix the cream and eggs yolk together. Add to the skillet and cook for 5 minutes over medium heat.
4. Add the chicken to the skillet and cook at low heat for 10 minutes.
5. While doing that, place the rice in boiled water until it's cooked (15 to 20 minutes).
6. Pre-heat oven to 375F and bake the puff shells for 20-25 minute until they become a golden color.
7. Take them out of the oven, fill with the chicken mixture, and surround with rice to serve.

Tips: you can replace the chicken with shrimp or fish.

Fricassee Chicken

What is fricassee? It's stew prepared without initially browning the meat. Though chicken is most commonly used in this type of stew, fish, vegetables, and other meats can be prepared in this manner as well.

Ingredients:
Serves 6

1 teaspoon seasoned salt
½ teaspoon black pepper
1 tablespoon steak sauce
1 tbsp. Worcestershire sauce
1 onion, finely chopped
3 cloves garlic, minced
6 pieces chicken (drumsticks, legs….)
2 tbsp. oil
2 cups water
½ lb chopped potatoes
¼ lb diced carrots

Preparation: 10 min + 30 min for marinade
Cooking: 45 min

1. Add seasoned salt, black pepper, garlic, steak sauce, Worcestershire sauce, and chopped onions to chicken in a bowl. Marinate for at least 30 minutes.
2. Place the chicken and marinade in a big skillet.
3. Add water, potatoes, and carrots
4. Cook on medium, covered, for 30 minutes. Simmer for 10 minutes.
5. Serve hot in gravy with rice or vegetables.

Jamaican Curried Chicken

Jamaican cuisine is a unique experience, featuring hints of Spanish, African, and Indian flavors. Elsewhere this dish would be known as chicken curry, but the Jamaicans call it curried chicken.

Ingredients:
Serves 4

1 lb Chicken (legs, thighs, or breasts
Lemon juice
2 tbsp. curry powder
1 onion chopped
2 cloves garlic
1 tbsp thyme
Salt and Black Pepper to taste
3 tbsp. oil

Preparation: 15 minutes
Cooking: 45 minutes

1. Clean the chicken with lemon juice.
2. In a medium bow, season the chicken with curry, onion, thyme, garlic, black pepper, and salt. Marinate for about 3 hours
3. Pour 3 tbsp. of oil into a skillet and cook the chicken and the marinade for 30 minutes to 1 hour over medium heat. Cooking time will depend on the size of the chicken pieces.

Tips: Serve over white rice.

Turkey Leg In Mustard Sauce

This recipe is so simple. You just need 2 hours to cook the turkey, with no preparation time. Try it – you won't be disappointed! You can also follow this recipe for a chicken

Ingredients:
Serves 4

1 onion, chopped
5 garlic cloves, chopped
2 branch of dried thyme
1 turkey leg
2 tbsp. mustard
3 tbsp. olive oil
6 oz red wine
1 glass of brandy
Salt and pepper
1 cup chicken broth

Preparation: 15 min
Cooking: 2 hours

1. Copped the onions and the garlic.
2. Put the turkey leg in an ovenproof pan and cover with mustard on each side. Salt and pepper to taste. Add onions, garlic, and thyme.
3. Pour chicken broth, red wine, brandy, and olive oil over the turkey.
4. Bake in the oven for 2 hours at 375 F

Szechuan Chicken

Szechuan cuisine originating in the Sichuan region of western china has an international reputation of being spicy and flavorful.

Ingredients:
Serves 4

4 boneless chicken breasts
2 tbsp sherry cooking wine
2 tbsp sesame oil
1 tbsp soy sauce
2 tbsp brown sugar
Dash cayenne pepper
1/2 tbsp crushed dried chilies
Dash salt and pepper
1 egg white
2 tsp cornstarch
Stir fry vegetables
Bamboo shoot

Preparation: 25 min
Cooking: 30 min

1. Cut chicken into small strips.
2. In a small bowl, combine sherry wine, sesame oil, soy sauce, sugar, cayenne pepper, and chilies. Set aside
3. In a different small bowl, mix egg whites and cornstarch.
4. Coat chicken in cornstarch mixture.
5. Heat wok.
6. Fry chicken legs until they turn white, for 10 to 15 minutes. Take the chicken out of the wok.
7. Place 1 tbsp. of oil in the wok, add bamboo and stir-fry vegetables and cook for 2 minutes.
8. Add sauce from the small bowl to the vegetables and cook for 10 to 20 minutes.
9. When the vegetables are cooked, add the chicken and cook another 15 minutes.

Arroz con Pollo

This is a popular Spanish dish, but you can also find it in Cuba and South America. It's yellow rice mixed with chicken, topped with melted cheese. This is one of my all time favorites

---

Ingredients:
Serves 4

3 chicken fillet
1 tablespoon steak sauce
1 tbsp Worcestershire sauce
1 onion, finely chopped
3 cloves garlic, minced
1 teaspoon seasoned salt
½ teaspoon black pepper
8 oz Yellow saffron rice
Shredded cheese (you can buy it in a bag at the supermarket with multiple types of cheese grated and mixed)

Preparation: 25 min
Cooking: 47 min

1. In a medium skillet, cook the chicken pieces with the steak sauce, Worcestershire sauce, onion, garlic, salt and pepper at medium heat for about 40 min.
2. Cook yellow rice as instructed on package
3. Mix chicken with rice in medium pot
4. Flatten top of chicken/rice mixture
5. Add hefty layer of shredded cheese
6. Cover pot and simmer for 7 minutes or until cheese is melted.

Rabbit in Mustard Sauce

Ingredients:
Serves 4

1/2 onion, chopped
1 garlic clove, chopped
1 rabbit
1 pot of French mustard or Dijon
1 tbsp. olive oil
2 glasses white wine
Few branches of dried thyme
Salt and pepper
2 tbsp sour cream (optional)

Preparation: 30 min
Cooking: 1 hour 1/2

1. Finely chop the onion and garlic. Cover the bottom of a large pot with 1 tbsp of olive oil. Add the onions and cook for several minutes until they soften.
2. Add rabbit pieces and garlic to the onions, and brown lightly.
3. Brush the rabbit with the mustard; add the wine, pepper, salt and thyme. Cover and let cook for approximately 1 hour and 30 minutes at low to medium heat.
4. Add more wine or mustard if needed.
5. To obtain a more creamy sauce, add 2 tbsp. sour cream.

Tips: Serve this dish with fresh tagliatelle or vegetables.

Canard A L'orange
(Duck with orange sauce)

This is a wonderful recipe for *canard a l'orange*. I'm sure you'll like it.

Ingredients:
Serves 6

3 large oranges
1 duck
3 tbsp oil
½ onion, sliced
2 carrots, sliced
5 oz white wine
0.33 fl oz orange liquor
Salt and pepper to taste

Preparation: 25 min
Cooking: 1 hour 30 min

1. Cut one of the oranges into thin slices and place orange slices inside the duck.
2. Brush the duck with oil, sprinkle with salt and pepper.
   Place the duck in a roasting tin and bake for 1 hour 15 minutes (depending on the size of the duck) at 375F.
3. After 15 minutes, add onions, carrots, and the wine.
4. Cook to a golden color.
5. Place the duck in a casserole with the orange liquor.
6. Moisten the roasting tin with a little water and pour the mixture over the duck.
7. Simmer for 15 minutes.
8. While the duck is cooking, cut the zest from the remaining two oranges and cut into thin strips
9. Blanch in boiling water and add to the duck.
10. You can serve this dish with slices of oranges fried in butter.

Duck with Pears And Raisins

Ingredients:
Serves 4

4 duck breasts or legs
2 tbsp olive oil
1 small onion, chopped
2 tbsp thyme
2 cups chicken broth
3 firm pears (ripe)
1 tbsp garlic
2 tbsp brandy
1 garlic clove
2 tbsp raisins
2 sticks cinnamon

Preparation: 25 min
Cooking: 1 hour 30 min

1. Place the duck breast and leg in a saucepan with 1 tbsp. olive oil and cook at medium heat until brown (about 5 to 8 minutes).
2. Place the onion, thyme, cinnamon, and chicken broth in a saucepan and bring to boil.
3. Pour over the duck the mixture, cover, and cook at low heat for 1 hour.
4. Peel and core the pears and fry them until golden colored. Add the raisins, crushed garlic, and the brandy.
5. Cook for another 10-15 minutes until the pears are cooked.
6. Place the duck pieces on a serving plate. Add the pears and raisins beside it for decoration and pour the gravy over the duck.

Tips: Serve this dish with mashed or boiled potatoes.

Caramelized Quails

Ingredients:
Serves 4

2 oz raspberry vinegar
3 bay leaves
20 oz oyster mushrooms
3 tbsp olive oil
3 garlic cloves
1 tbsp thyme
4 bay leaves
Salt and pepper to taste
3.5 oz butter
5 oz honey
4 quails (boneless)
½ cup chicken broth

Preparation: 25 minutes + 2 hours for marinade
Cooking: 30 min

1. Bring the raspberry vinegar to a boil along with bay leaves.
2. Add the mushrooms and cook on low heat for 15 minutes.
3. In small bowl, make a marinade with the olive oil, crushed garlic, thyme, bay leaves, salt, and pepper. Spread over the quail.
4. Let rest for one or two hours.
5. In a skillet, melt the butter and the honey and fry the quail for about 15 minutes.
6. Place the quail in an ovenproof dish and cook at 375 F for about 3 minutes.
7. Then add the vinegar, marinade, and the broth. Let cook slowly for 20 minutes.

Curried Shrimp

Ingredients:
Serves 4

1 onion
2 cloves garlic, minced
3 tbsp oil
2 tbsp curry powder
1 lb. fresh shrimp, cleaned and de-veined
2 tsp lemon juice
1 tbsp butter
Salt and pepper to taste

Preparation: 10 min
Cooking: 5 min

1. Sauté chopped onions and minced garlic in oil. Add curry.
2. After approximately 2 minutes, add shrimp, salt, and pepper. Cook shrimp for 5 minutes while stirring.
3. Mix in lemon juice and butter. The shrimp should be firm, but tender.

Tips: Serve with pasta or over rice, with a tossed salad.

Saffron Salmon

Ingredients:
Serves 4

4 salmon fillets
2 tbsp butter
½ cup whipped cream
0.1 oz saffron
1 leek sliced finely (white part)
1 carrot, sliced
1 tbsp oil
1/2 cup brandy
3.5 Oz shrimp, peeled
1 garlic clove, crushed
Parsley, finely chopped, as a garnish
Salt and pepper to taste

Preparation: 30 min
Cooking: 25 min

1. In a skillet, cook the salmon with the butter for 15-25 minutes.
2. In a saucepan, cook the leek and carrot with 1 tbsp of oil. Once the vegetables are cooked, add cream, the saffron, and salt and pepper to taste.
3. Pour ¼ cup brandy over the salmon and cook for 7 minutes.
4. Place the shrimp in a skillet and cook with the garlic for 2 minutes.
5. Pour ¼ cup brandy into a small saucepan and warm it. Light the brandy, pour it over the shrimp, and cook for 3 minutes.
6. Place the salmon in the center of a plate and cover with the sauce. Garnish with parsley.
7. Place the shrimp around the plate.

Tips: Serve with chilled white wine (Chardonnay, Chablis).

Grilled Garlic Lobster

This is the first dish my husband cooked for me (he is an excellent cook)! It's absolutely stunning!

Ingredients:
Serves 2

2 lobsters
12 oz butter
2 garlic cloves
1 shallot
Salt and pepper to taste
1 tbsp. fresh basil

Preparation: 20 min
Cooking: 20 min

1. Get a large pot with a lid and put water on to boil.
2. When water is boiling, add a live lobster. (Be careful of the claws)!
3. Cover with a lid as soon as the lobster is in water. When water start to boil again, time it for 7 minutes. Rinse the boiled lobster.
4. Split the tails lengthwise along the back
5. Twist off the head from the tail. Remove liver, roe, and stomach.
6. Release flesh from tails, keeping the end still attached. Remove the intestinal vein beneath flesh of center back, rinse, and return to shell.
7. Season lightly with salt and pepper
8. Melt the butter with garlic and shallots and brush the lobster with it.
9. Turn broiler to medium heat and place halves of lobsters, meat side up, on the broiler rack. Leave it for 3-4 minutes.
10. Heat remainder of butter and pour over the lobster before serving. Sprinkle with fresh basil.

Scallops with White Wine Sauce

Ingredients:
Serves 4

1 tbsp butter
½ cup onion, chopped
2 cloves garlic
1 cup white wine
1 tbsp. fresh parsley, chopped
1 tomato, diced
¾ cup heavy cream
½ lb sea scallop
Dash of saffron
Salt and pepper to taste

Preparation: 20 min
Cooking: 20 min

Sauce
1. In a skillet, melt the butter and cook the onion and garlic until soft.
2. Add the wine and bring to a simmer
3. Add the parsley, tomato, cream, and salt and pepper.
4. Cook for 20 minutes on low-medium heat.
5. Cook the scallops in a different skillet with 1 tbsp. olive oil and a dash of saffron until they are browned.
6. Serve over pasta

Mussels In Beer Sauce

This is a Belgium recipe! Serve with French fries and beer.

Ingredients:
Serves 4

2 onions
1 shallot
1 oz butter
100 oz clean mussels
1 bottle beer
2 tbsp. flour
1 egg yolk
3.5 oz cream
Salt and pepper to taste
1 tbsp fresh parsley, chopped

Preparation: 10 minutes
Cooking: 10 minutes

1. Chop the onions and the shallot and place in a saucepan with 1 tbsp. butter. Cook until golden in color. Add the beer, salt, and pepper to taste.
2. Add the mussels and cook for 5 minutes.
3. Filter the sauce and put it in a saucepan.
4. Add the rest of the butter and the flour. Stir until you obtain a thick mixture.
5. Mix the egg yolk and cream and add it to the rest of the sauce. Stir and pour over the mussels. Add salt and pepper to taste
6. Cook for 5 minutes and serve. The mussels must be well open.
7. Sprinkle with fresh parsley.

Salmon Pasta Gratin

Ingredients:
Serves 4

1 lbs penne pasta
2 small leeks
1 clove garlic
½ red onion, chopped
0.8 oz butter
2 tbsp flour
¾ cup white wine
20 oz crème fraiche or sour cream
1 tbsp Lemon juice
4 slices smoked or fresh salmon
6 oz Parmesan cheese
Salt and pepper

Preparation: 30 minutes
Cooking: 20 minutes

1. Cook pasta in boiling water for about 15 minutes (salt the water and add a spoon of oil). When cooked, drain in a colander, then return the pasta to the pot and toss with the butter.
2. While the pasta is cooking, clean and cut the leek into small pieces and cook at low heat in a spoonful of olive oil with salt and pepper, garlic, and red onion.
3. While the pasta and the leek are cooking, we will prepare the sauce:
4. Melt the butter in a saucepan with 2 tbsp. flour. As it thickens, add the white wine you've diluted in a glass of hot water. Cook at low to medium heat, stirring until you obtain a thick paste. Add the crème fraiche and a little bit of lemon juice. Add salt and pepper to taste
5. Place half the pasta in an oven-safe dish and spread half of the leek mixture on top. Add half of the sauce and cover with the salmon. Repeat this step with the second half of the pasta.
6. Bake in the oven at 375 F for 15 to 20 minutes.

Spicy Red Snapper

Ingredients:
Serves 4

1 tbsp parsley, minced
1 tbsp paprika
1/8 tbsp cayenne
Dash of oregano
Dash of black pepper and salt
4 red snapper fillets
1 tbsp butter
1/4 onion chopped
1 garlic clove
2 tbsp lemon juice
3 branches of thyme

Preparation: 15 minutes
Cooking: 20 minutes

1. Mix all the spices together (parsley, paprika, cayenne, oregano, pepper and salt), and sprinkle over each side of the fish.
2. Add salt and pepper to taste
3. Place the fillets in a skillet with one tbsp. butter.
4. Add the onion, garlic, and lemon.
5. Add the thyme.
6. Cook at medium heat for about 20 minutes.

Garlic Mashed Potatoes

Ingredients:
Serves 4

4 potatoes
2 tbsp butter
1 garlic clove cut in 4ths
1 egg
1/4 cup milk
½ cup grated cheese
Salt and pepper to taste

Preparation: 5 minutes
Cooking: 15 minutes

1. Cook potatoes in boiling water until they become soft.
2. In a small saucepan, melt the butter and cook the garlic at medium heat until soft, remove the garlic.
3. When the potatoes are cooked, mash them.
4. Add the butter to the potatoes.
5. Beat the egg and add it to the potatoes, add the milk, and grated cheese.
6. Add salt and pepper to taste.

Tip: Add more or less milk, depending on how tick you want the mashed potatoes.

Ratatouille

Originally from the Provence region in southern France, ratatouille can be served with any type of meat or fish.

Ingredients:
Serves 4

2 eggplants
6 zucchini
1 large onion
2 to 4 cloves garlic
2 tbsp. olive oil
8 fresh tomatoes
¼ cup white wine
Salt and pepper

Preparation: 20 min
Cooking: 30-45 min

1. Wash the eggplant and zucchini.
2. Cut the eggplant into small cubes and slice the zucchini into slices.
3. Chop the onion and crush the garlic.
4. In a saucepan, put 2 tbsp. of oil and add the onions and sauté until golden brown. Add the eggplant, zucchini, and garlic and cook until golden
5. Stir and add the tomatoes and wine.
6. Cover and simmer for 30 to 45 minutes. Add salt and pepper to taste.

The Garden Dish

Ingredients:
Serves 4

2 potatoes, cut in small pieces
2 carrots, sliced
2 slice of salted pork cut in pieces
1 oz green beans
1 tbsp butter
1 clove garlic
¼ onion
4 oz peas
Salt and pepper to taste

Preparation: 15 minutes
Cooking: 30 minutes

1. Clean and cut the potatoes, carrot, salted pork, and green beans in small pieces.
2. In a skillet, melt 1 tbsp. butter and saute the salted pork, garlic and onion until soft.
3. Add all the vegetables and cook for about 30 minutes until all vegetable are cooked.
4. Add salt and pepper to taste

Potatoes Gratin

Ingredients:
Serves 4

2lb potatoes, sliced
1 red pepper, sliced
½ onion, chopped
2 cloves garlic, chopped
¼ cup grated Gruyere or
Parmesan cheese
Ground nutmeg (optional)
Salt and pepper
1 cup milk
1 cup whipped cream

Preparation: 15 min
Cooking: 45 min

1. Preheat the oven at 375 F for 15 minutes.
2. Butter a baking pan.
3. In a medium bowl, mix sliced potatoes, peppers, the onions and garlic, half of the cheese, salt and pepper, and the nutmeg.
4. Place the mixture in a baking pan.
5. In a small bowl, mix the milk and cream and pour it over the potatoes
6. Top with the remaining cheese.
7. Bake for about 45 minutes at 375 F.

Stuffed Tomatoes

Ingredients:
Serves 4

5 oz ground turkey or beef
Dash cayenne pepper
1 tbsp. dried thyme
1 tbsp. oil
1 garlic clove
2 oz. mushrooms
1 red pepper
1 onion
1 tbsp chili powder
Salt and pepper to taste
4 big tomatoes
1 cup rice
1 cup of chicken broth

Preparation: 20 minutes
Cooking: 35 minutes

1. In a large skillet, heat oil and cook the ground turkey with cayenne pepper, thyme, garlic, mushrooms, red pepper, onion, chili powder, salt, and pepper. Cook for 15-20 minutes at medium heat.
2. Cut tops off tomatoes about 3/4" down from top. Save them. Using a spoon, scoop out insides of tomatoes, leaving outer layer intact.
3. Place the tomatoes in a baking dish
4. Stuff the tomatoes with the meat.
5. Place the rice around the tomatoes and add a cup of chicken broth to the rice
6. Bake for 35 min at 375 F (until the rice is cooked).

Parmesan Zucchini

Ingredients:
Serves 4

4 to 5 medium zucchini, about 1 1/2 lbs
1/4 cup all-purpose flour
1 tbsp dried oregano
1/2 tbsp dried basil
½ tbsp dried thyme
1/4 cup olive oil
1/2 cup grated Parmesan cheese
Salt and pepper to taste

Preparation: 15 minutes
Cooking: 10-15 minutes

1. Peel and cut the zucchini into slices.
2. In a small bowl. Mix the flour with the oregano, basil, Parmesan, thyme, salt, and pepper.
3. Coat the zucchini into the flour mixture
4. In large skillet, heat oil over medium heat and cook the zucchini until golden brown on each side (approximately 5 minutes).

Tortellini with Spinach

Ingredients:
Serves 4

1 package tortellini
1 package baby spinach chopped
½ cup chicken broth
¼ onion, chopped fine
1 clove garlic
1 medium tomato, chopped
½ tsp ground nutmeg
1 tbsp fresh basil
3 oz. chopped walnuts
2 tbsp olive oil
2 tbsp sour cream
1 cup powdered Parmesan cheese
Salt and pepper to taste

Preparation: 20 min
Cooking: 20 min

1. Boil water to cook the tortellini. Add one pinch of salt to the water and cook for 8-10 minutes.
2. In a medium saucepan add the baby spinach, the chicken broth, onion, garlic, tomato, nutmeg, basil, walnut, salt and pepper to taste, and 2 tbsp olive oil. Cook for 15-20 minutes over medium heat. Add the sour cream and cook for another 5 minutes.
3. Drain the tortellini. Place the spinach mix in a serving plate and top with the tortellini. Sprinkle with Parmesan cheese.

Spanish Tortilla

I got this recipe from my friend Yolanda, who's from Spain. It 's so good I can never make enough!

Ingredients:
Serves 4

1/4 cup olive oil
4 large potatoes, peeled and slice
One large onion, thinly Sliced
4 eggs
Salt and pepper to taste

Preparation: 20 minutes
Cooking: 20 minute

1. Heat oil in a large, non-stick frying pan.
2. Alternate layers of potato and onions. Cook slowly, at low to medium heat until potatoes are tender.
3. Beat the eggs in a large bowl. Add salt and pepper to taste. Add the potatoes and onions to the bowl.
4. Heat the pan again and add the mixture. Cook for about 4 to 6 minutes on medium high heat. Shake pan to prevent sticking.
5. Cover the pan with a plate and invert the omelet into it. Slide it back into the pan and cook for another 4-6 minutes. You can repeat this action 2 to 3 times for better cooking
6. You can also add some red pepper for additional flavor

Salt Fish and Fried Dumplings

This is a traditional recipe from Jamaica

Ingredients:

Serves 4

2 cups self-rising four
1 1/2 cups of water
Dash of salt
8 oz salt fish (salted codfish) soaked overnight
2 large tomatoes sliced
1 garlic clove chopped
1 onion Chopped
6 oz sliced mushrooms

Preparation: 15 minutes
Cooking: 10 minutes

For the dumplings

1. In a small bowl, sift the flour and the salt together.
2. Add the water slowly, just enough to make a firm dough
3. Add a dash of salt.
4. Heat oil in a frying pan over medium heat.
5. Form the dough into small biscuit and fry them for 2-3 minutes on both until golden.

For the salt fish

6. In a skillet heat 1 tbsp. of oil and cook onion and garlic until soft.
7. Add the tomatoes, mushroom, and salt fish and cook another 5 minutes.
   Serve with the dumplings.

Grated Cauliflower

You should try this recipe; you won't even recognize its cauliflower!

Ingredients:
Serves 4

2 cauliflower heads
1 tbsp butter
½ onion, Chopped
2 garlic cloves
2 slices of salted pork (if you can't find salted pork, use bacon)
Salt and pepper to taste
½ cup Grated cheese

Preparation: 10 minutes
Cooking: 25 minutes

1. Boil a pot of water with 1 tbsp of salt and cook the cauliflower for about 20 minutes (until soft).
2. Melt the butter in a skillet and cook onion, garlic and salted pork for 5-7minutes over medium heat
3. Pour the cauliflower into the skillet and cook for 2-3 minutes.
4. Place the mixture in an ovenproof dish and top with grated cheese.
5. Broil for few minutes.

Potato Pancakes

Ingredients:
Serves 4

2 eggs
2 tsp. oil
3 potatoes, shredded
2 tbsp milk
2 tbsp dried parsley
1 garlic cloves
½ onion, finely chopped
Salt and pepper to taste

Preparation: 15 minutes
Cooking: 15 minutes

1. In a small bowl, whisk eggs and mix with milk, salt, and pepper.
2. Add the onion, garlic, and potatoes. Mix well.
3. Heat the oil in a skillet.
4. With your hand, make little pancakes (4-inches) and place them in the skillet.
5. Cook over medium heat, turning once, until brown on both sides.

Cheese Plateaux
(Cheese Platter)

Composition:

Brie
Goat cheese
Gruyere or emmental
Cheddar
Blue cheese (ex:
Danish blue)
Almond
Grapes
Pear
Baguette or country
bread

Red wine (Bordeaux,
Beaujolais or Merlot)

Desserts

Fresh Fruits Salad

Fruits salad is perfect in the summer, but also at the end of a big meal. You can change the fruit in this recipe to match the season.

Ingredients:
Serves 4

2 thinly sliced, unpeeled apples
1 cup seedless green or red grapes
1 sliced banana
1 can pineapple chunks, drained
1 cup cantaloupe, cut up
1 kiwifruit, peeled and sliced
1 slice watermelon
1 tbsp lemon juice
1 tbsp. rum
2 tbsp. sugar

Preparation: 15 minutes

1. Clean and cut all the fruits in a medium bowl
2. Mix 1 tbsp lemon juice with 1 tbsp of rum and pour it over the fruits.
3. Sprinkle with sugar.
4. Let stand for 1 hour in the refrigerator.

Apple Crumble

Ingredients:

Serves 6-8

¾ cup flour
4 tbsp sugar
1 dash salt
½ cup butter cut in small pieces
1 ½ tbsp melted butter
6 apples
5 tbsp sugar
1 tbsp vanilla
¼ cup raisins
3 tbsp chopped, blanched almonds
3 tbsp brandy
1 tbsp cinnamon
1 tsp butter for the pan

Preparation: 25 minutes
Baking: 25 minutes

1. Pour the flour into a medium bowl. Add the 4 tbsp sugar and dash of salt. Add ½ cup of butter cut in small pieces
2. Mix with the tip of the fingers until a crumbly mass has formed. Refrigerate for 30 minutes.
3. Peel and dice the apples.
4. In a skillet, melt 1 ½ tbsp of butter. Add the apples, the sugar and the vanilla flavoring.
5. Cook at medium heat until the apples turn into a puree.
6. Add the raisins and almonds.
7. Heat up the brandy and light it on fire before pouring it over the apples.
8. Let cook for 20 minutes at low heat.
9. Grease a pie dish. Put the apple puree into it and sprinkle with cinnamon.
10. Sprinkle the crumble over the puree.
11. Bake for 25 minutes.

Clafoutis

A dessert of fruit, originally cherries, covered with a thick batter and baked until puffy. This wonderful dessert can be served hot or cold.

Ingredients:
Serves 6-8

2. ½ cup cherries
4 eggs
1/2 cup sugar
1/2 cup all purpose flour
1 pint of milk
1 tbsp vanilla
Dash of salt

Preparation: 25 minutes
Baking: 45 minutes

1. Pre-heat the oven to 375 F.
2. Take the seeds from the cherries, remove the stalk, and clean the cherries.
3. In a medium bowl, beat the eggs and add sugar. Stir well.
4. Add the flour.
5. Add the milk little by little, without stopping to stir.
6. Add the vanilla and the salt.
7. Grease a pie dish and place the cherries on it.
8. Pour the mixture over the cherries
9. Bake for 45 minutes at 375 F.

Tips: Instead of fresh cherries, you can substitute plums, pears, peaches, apples, or any other fruit.

Apple Tart

Nothing more delicious than a simple apple tart. I love it! This is easy to make and so delicious.

Ingredients:
Serves 6-8

6 large Granny Smith
apples
1 pie crust
1 egg
1 cup milk
3 tbsp sugar
1 1/2 tsp vanilla flavoring
1 lemon
Dash of cinnamon powder

Preparation: 20 minutes
Baking: 40 minutes

1. Peel, core, and slice the apples.
2. Place the crust in a pie dish and fill it with apple slices/
3. Beat eggs with cream, sugar, vanilla, and lemon, and until foamy.
4. Pour over apples.
5. Sprinkle cinnamon powder over the apples.
6. Bake for 40 minutes at medium heat or until brown.

Blueberry, Raspberry and Strawberry Cheesecake

Ingredients:
Serves 6-8

3 packages cream cheese
(8 oz total.)
1 cup sugar
3 eggs
1 tsp vanilla
1 pie crust (graham cracker
crust)
1 cup frozen or fresh
blueberries
1 cup frozen or fresh
raspberries
1 cup strawberries

Preparation: 20 minutes
Baking: 45 minutes

1. In a blender, combine cream cheese and sugar at medium speed until well blended.
2. Add eggs (one at a time)
3. Mix well after each addition.
4. Blend in vanilla.
5. Pour mixture into the crust.
6. Bake for 45 min at 375 F.
7. Let cool.
8. Unfreeze the blueberry; raspberry and strawberry; top the cake with them.

French Toast With Fruits

There are a number of conflicting stories about the origin of French toast, also known as, "*pain perdu*" or "lost bread," it is actually made with day-old bread.

Ingredients:
Serves 6

3 eggs
2 apples cut in small cubes
10 walnuts
2 cup of milk
6 tbsp. sugar
1/2 glass of rum
10 slices French bread
¼ of cup of raisins

Preparation: 10 minutes
Baking: 20 minutes

1. Pour the eggs, apples, walnuts, milk, sugar, and rum into a food processor and blend for 30 seconds.
2. Grease an ovenproof dish and place the bread slices on the bottom of the dish.
3. Pour the mixture over the bread.
4. Sprinkle the raisins on top.
5. Bake for 15 minutes at 375 F.
6. Broil for 5 minutes at 400 F.

Banana Banoffi

Invented at the Hungry Monk in 1972, Banoffi Pie is still as popular today as it was the first time it appeared on the menu. There have been many imitations as far and wide as Russia and the United States; it is even rumored to be Mrs. Thatcher's favorite pudding!

Ingredients:
Serves 6-8

Pie Shell:

9 oz (1 package) ginger biscuits, crushed
½ cup butter
Whipped topping and chocolate powder to decorate

For the Toffee:

1 can condensed milk
¾ cup butter
3 tbsp brown sugar
2 bananas
6-7 strawberries

Preparation: 25 minutes

Pie Shell:

1. Crush the ginger biscuits and add melted butter.
2. Pour the mix into a pie plate, press down to form a crust, and refrigerate for 30 minutes.

For the Toffee:

1. Melt the butter; add the brown sugar and the condensed milk and heat for about 7 minutes.
2. Stir until mixture turns a golden caramel color.
3. Let cool for a few minutes, then pour into the pie shell. Refrigerate for at least an hour.
4. Before serving the banana banoffi, slice the bananas and strawberries and arrange them on top of the toffee. Spread whipped topping over the mixture and decorate with grated chocolate on top.

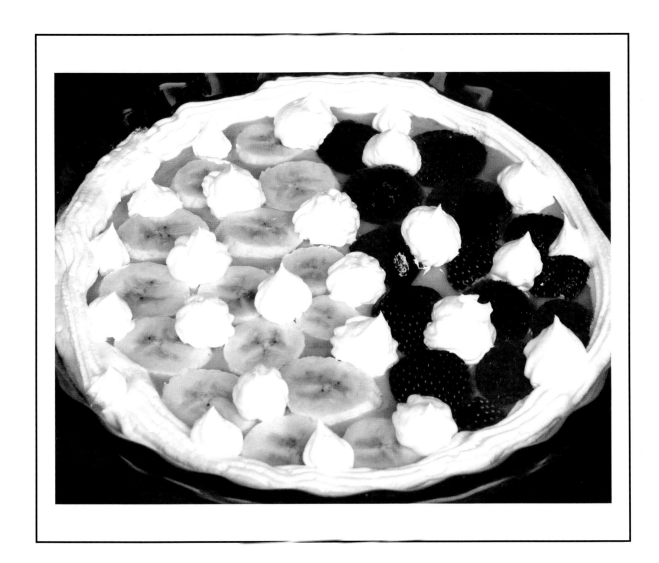

Cantaloupe Ice Cream in Almond Sauce

Ingredients:
Serves 6

1 1/2 cantaloupe (pick a sweet one)
1 cup milk
1 cup heavy cream
½ cup honey
½ lemon
1 tbsp vanilla essence

Sauce:
3 tbsp almonds
2 tbsp of honey
7 tbsp of whipped cream

Preparation: 15 minutes

1. Cut the melon into small pieces. Add the milk, cream, honey, lemon, and vanilla.
2. Blend all together. (In a blender)
3. Pour into a dish.
4. Refrigerate for 15 minutes, then place in the freezer for at least 3 to 4 hours. Overnight is even better.

Sauce:
Place the almonds in a skillet. Heat for few minutes and then add the honey. Let caramelized for few minutes and add the cream.

Floating Island

This dessert is also called *"oeufs a la neige."* It's soft vanilla custard with floating clouds of meringue. Delicious!

Ingredients:
Serves 4

4 eggs yolks
¼ cup white sugar
1 ½ cups warm whole milk
1 tbsp vanilla flavoring
1 tbsp rum

For the Meringue

5 egg whites
4 tbsp superfine sugar

Preparation: 15 minutes

Sauce
1. In a small bowl, mix the egg yolks with sugar for about 5 minutes
2. In a saucepan warm the milk, vanilla, and rum and until boiling.
3. Add the milk to the egg yolk very slowly.
4. Pour in a pan and cook for about 5 to 10 minutes until the mixture begins to thicken.
5. Beat egg whites with an electric mixer until stiff and add the superfine sugar.
6. Boil water in a saucepan. With a spoon, scoop up some egg white and put it in the boiling water. Boil on one side, and then the other.
7. Drain the egg whites on kitchen paper.
8. Place the egg whites on top of the cream and cover with caramel sauce.

Crème Brulee

Crème brulee is one of the most popular desserts in the world today! Try this recipe: it's easy and you won't have to go to the restaurant to have a crème brulee anymore. You can enjoy it at home

Ingredients:
Serves 4-6

5 egg yolks
6 tbsp of white sugar
2 cups heavy cream
3 tbsp granulated sugar
1 tbsp pure vanilla extract

Preparation: 25 minutes
Baking: 45 minutes

1. In a medium-sized bowl, whisk the egg yolks and cream.
2. Add 6 tbsp. sugar and vanilla extract.
3. Pour the mixture into four ramekins, or custard cups. Place the ramekins in a 9 x 13-inch baking pan. Pour water into the pan (do not allow any water to fall into the ramekins) until the ramekins are sitting in 1 to 1-1/2 inches of water.
4. Bake for 45 minutes.
5. Sprinkle 1 tsp. of the remaining sugar over each ramekin. Return to the oven and place under the broiler until sugar has caramelized.

Coconut Flan With Caramel

Ingredients:
Serves 4

1/4 cup sugar
1/4 cup hot water
1 cup fresh or canned
Coconut milk
1 cup milk
1/4 cup sugar
4 eggs
1 tbsp vanilla extract

Preparation: 20 minutes
Cooking: 30 minutes

1. In a small saucepan, mix the sugar and the water and cook over low heat until you obtain a brown color.
2. Pour the caramel into ramekins (custard dishes). Tilt the molds to coat all the surfaces with caramel.
3. In a saucepan, combine the coconut milk, sugar, and milk. Cook over low heat for 10minutes.
4. Whisk the eggs and vanilla in a bowl. Add the coconut milk mixture and stir well.
5. Pour the mixture into the ramekins.
6. Cook in the oven in a bain-marie. (Place the ramekins in a 9 x 13-inch baking pan. Pour water into the pan, but do not allow any water to fall into the ramekins. Add water until ramekins are sitting in 1 to 1-1/2 inches of water). Bake for about 30 minutes at 375 F. (do not let the water boil).

White Chocolate Mousse

Ingredients:
Serves 6

16 oz white chocolate
1 cup heavy whipping cream
3 eggs, separated
1/4 cup hot water
1/4 cup brandy
4 tbsp sugar
1 tbsp vanilla

Chocolate sauce:

2 ounce of semisweet chocolate
2 tbsp of dark rum
¼ cup light cream

Preparation: 25 minutes

1. Melt the white chocolate in a double boiler over low heat. Stir until it's completely melted.

2. Whip the cream and set aside.
3. In a medium bowl, whisk the egg yolk, the hot water and the brandy. (Make sure it's well mixed).
4. Add the melted chocolate and keep whisking for 5 to 10 minutes.
5. Beat egg whites with electric mixer until stiff and add 4 tbsp of sugar and the vanilla.
6. Carefully fold the egg whites into the chocolate mixture with a wooden spoon. Let cool.
7. Fold in the whipped cream. Warning! The chocolate mixture must be cool or the whipped cream will break apart.

Sauce:
8. Melt the chocolate with the rum and the cream in a saucepan Cook until the chocolate is completely melted.

Chocolate Muffins

Ingredients:
For 10 muffins

1.5 cup all purpose flour
2 tbsp of oil
1/2 cup of granulated sugar
1.5 tbsp of baking powder
1 cup of milk
2 eggs
1 tbsp vanilla flavoring
1 cup chocolate chips

Preparation: 15 minutes
Cooking: 20 minutes

1. Pre-heat the oven at 375 F.
2. Grease a muffin pan.
3. Mix the flour, oil, sugar, and baking powder together.
4. Add the milk, eggs and the vanilla and stir.
5. Add the chocolate chips. Pour the mixture into the muffin pan, filling each section half way.
6. Cook for 20-25 minutes at 375F.

Tips: You can replace the chocolate chips with blueberries, raisins, or hazelnuts.

Red Fruits and Nutella Crepes

Ingredients:
For 20 crepes

1 cup all purpose flour
4 eggs
1/2 cup melted butter
2 cup milk
3 tbsp dark rum
1 tbsp oil
1 dash of salt
1 pot of nutella (chocolate hazelnut spread)
6 strawberry
½ lb blueberry
½ lb raspberry

Preparation: 25 minutes

1. Mix the flour and eggs in a medium bowl.
2. Add the melted butter
3. Add the salt, milk, and rum.
4. Let rest for an hour.
5. Heat a 7- to 8-inch crepe pan over moderate heat and brush lightly with oil.
6. Tilt the pan to coat the bottom with a thin layer of batter and pour off the excess.
7. Cook the crepe for about 30 seconds on each side, until lightly browned.
8. Keep the crepe warm.
9. Fill the crepe with 1 tbsp. of nutella and the sliced fruit.

You can also serve the crepe still warm with vanilla ice cream.

Easter Spice Bun

This is a traditional Jamaican recipe. A bun is a sweet spicy cake, and this recipe is usually served at Easter with cheese.

Ingredients:
Serves 6-8

1 egg
2 cups brown sugar
1 tbsp butter
1 cup milk
1 tbsp nutmeg
1 tbsp cinnamon
4 tbsp baking powder
3 cups all purpose flour
2 tbsp lime juice
Dash of salt
1 cup raisins and/or dried fruit

Preparation: 25 minutes
Cooking: 1 hour

1. Preheat oven to 350 F for 15 minutes.
2. Beat egg and add sugar, melted butter and milk.
3. Add the nutmeg, cinnamon, baking powder, flour, limejuice, and a dash of salt. Beat until smooth.
4. Add raisins or dried fruit
5. Pour into lined and greased loaf pan and bake for about an hour at 375F.
6. When the bun is baked, make a glaze with ½ cup brown sugar and ½ cup water that you bring to boil until thick. Spread the glaze over the bun.
7. Put back the bun in the oven for 5 minutes.

Chocolate Cake

Ingredients:
Serves 8-10

1 cup butter
½ cup sugar
4 eggs
½ cup flour
8 oz dark chocolate
2 tbsp baking powder
2 tbsp vanilla extract
¼ cup ground almonds
3/4 cup grated coconut

Preparation: 20 minutes
Baking: 45 minutes

1. Preheat oven 375 F.
2. In a large bowl, mix the melted butter with sugar.
3. Add one egg at a time and mix well.
4. Add the flour, melted dark chocolate, baking powder, vanilla extract, ground almonds, and grated coconut.
5. Add ½ cup of boiling water and mix well.
6. Pour the mixture into a cake pan and bake for 45 minutes at 375F.

Hazelnut and Carrot Cake

Ingredients:
Serves 6-8

1 cup carrots, grated
1 lemon
4 eggs
1 cup of sugar
½ cup hazelnuts powder
¼ cup all purpose flour
1 pinch of salt
1 tbsp baking powder

Preparation: 20 minutes
Cooking: 45 minutes

1. Clean and grate the carrots.
2. Clean the lemon and grate it, keeping the zest.
3. Separate the eggs, placing the yolks in a bowl. Keep the egg whites on the side.
4. Add sugar to the egg yolks and mix well
5. Add the lemon zest, carrot, hazelnut powder, flour, salt, and baking powder.
6. Beat egg whites with electric mixer until stiff.
7. Add the stiff peaks to the rest of the mixture, delicately mixing.
8. Pour the preparation into a greased baking pan and bake for 45 minutes at 375 F.
9. Let cool before eating it.

Brownies

Americans have enjoyed brownies since the 19th century. They are a perfect blend of cookie and cake; perfect with a cup of tea or coffee.

Ingredients:

1/2 cup flour
1/4 tsp baking powder
1/8 tsp salt
1/2 cup butter
1 cup sugar
1/2 tsp vanilla extract
1 tbsp brandy
2 eggs
2 squares unsweetened chocolate
1 cup chopped walnuts or pecans

Preparation: 20 minutes
Cooking: 30 minutes

1. Grease and flour an 8-inch square-baking pan.
2. In a small bowl sift together flour, baking powder, and salt.
3. In a mixing bowl, beat butter, sugar, vanilla, brandy and egg together until light and fluffy.
4. Add melted chocolate
5. Pour in flour mixture, and then fold in the chopped nuts.
6. Spread brownie batter in prepared pan; bake for 25 to 30 minutes at 375 F
7. Cut brownies into squares while still warm; cool before removing from pan.

Tip: Brownies can be plain, iced, or served with ice cream and chocolate sauce.

Black Forest

This cake from Germany was originally called *Schwarzwaelder Kirschtorte.* Each time I make this dessert my guests are amazed.

Ingredients:
Serves 8-10

4 eggs
1 cup flour all purpose
1 cup of sugar
2 tbsp of sugar
½ cup unsalted butter
1 ½ tsp baking powder
1/4 cup of cocoa
1 tbsp. vanilla extract
15 oz. can black cherries, pitted and Drained, liquid reserved
3-4 tbsp kirsch or brandy

Preparation: 25 minutes
Baking: 45 minutes

1. Marinade the cherries with the kirsch (or brandy) for about 2 hours.
2. In a bowl beat, the egg yolk with 3 tbsp. of hot water. Add 1 cup of sugar little by little. Add the vanilla.
3. Beat egg whites with an electric mixer until stiff and add 2 tbsp of sugar. Add this to the egg yolks.
4. Add the flour, cocoa and baking powder and mix gently.
5. Add the melted butter.
6. Pour the mixture into a greased baking pan. (8 x 1-1/2-inch round baking pans)
7. Cook for 45 min at 375 F. Don't cook more than 45 minutes or the edges will be hard.
8. Let the cake cool, and then cut it in half horizontally and separate.
9. Pour just a little bit of kirsch over the bottom half of the cake. Add the cherries and cover with the whipped cream.
10. Replace the top half of the cake, cover with remaining cherries, and cover with whipped cream. Use grated chocolate for decoration.

Tip: you can decorate the cake with strawberries instead of cherries.

Tarte Tatin

This upside-down tart is a traditional dish of central France. As the story goes, it's a tart that was accidentally flipped over and then served to the parish priest. Serve the tart warm with vanilla ice cream.

Ingredients:
Serves 6-8

½ cup unsalted butter
½ cup of white sugar
4-5 apples, peeled, cored and cut into wedges
1 tbsp lemon juice
Dash cinnamon
1 pastry crust

Preparation: 20 minutes
Baking: 30 minutes

1. Melt the butter in a pie dish over medium heat and add sugar.
2. Gently stir until sugar starts to turn brown, about 3 to 5 minutes. Do not burn it.
3. Place apple halves in the dish, round side down, until the dish is full of apples.
4. Sprinkle with lemon juice and a little bit of cinnamon
5. Top the apples with the pastry crust and tuck the edges of the pastry around the sides of the tin.
6. Bake for 30-40 minutes at 375 F.

Mille-feuille With Apples, Calvados And Wild Berries

Ingredients:
Serves 4-6

18 oz of puff pastry
1 egg yolk
3 apples
1/2 cup of sugar
2 tbsp calvados or brandy
½ cup of wild berries
½ cup white wine
3 tbsp of berry syrup
½ cup Whipped topping

Preparation: 15 minutes
Baking: 5 minutes

1. With a glass, make 8 discs with the puff pastry.
2. Brush each puff with egg yolk so it takes a golden color
3. Bake at 200 degrees for 5-10 minutes.
4. Peel and slice the apples. Stir fry the apples with the sugar and brandy

For the sauce:
5. Mix the wild berries with white wine and the syrup

To prepare the cake:
Place the sauce in a dessert plate.
Top with 4 disc of puff fill discs of puff pastry with the apples and cover with the other 4 puff pastry disc. Place whipped topping on top and decorate with wild berries.

Raspberry Charlotte

Ingredients:

Serve: 4

40 lady fingers
1 ¼ cup whipped topping
2 1/2 cup raspberry
3 tbsp. raspberry syrup

Preparation: 10 minutes

1. In a medium bowl, mix 2 glasses of water with 3 tbsp. raspberry syrup.
2. Take 3 ramekins and pass them under cold water (do not dry them). Moisten the ladyfingers in the water-syrup mix (just enough to wet them but not too much) and place them on the bottom and around the ramekins. Follow with a layer of whipped topping and a layer of raspberry.
3. Repeat this action until you reach the top of the ramekin.
4. Chill overnight and then turn onto a serving plate.

Tips: You can replace the raspberries with any fruit, such as strawberries, mango, blueberries, or cherries. I used Nutella for the decoration

Fudge Mocha

Ingredients:
Serves 4-6

½ cup evaporated milk
2 tbsp butter
1 cup sugar
1 tbsp strong coffee
½ cup marshmallows
8 tbsp grated chocolate
1 tbsp. vanilla flavoring
1 ½ tbsp ground walnuts

Preparation: 20 minutes

1. In a saucepan, combine the milk, butter, sugar and coffee. Bring to a boil while stirring. Let boil for 4 to 5 minutes and take off the heat.
2. Add the marshmallow, chocolate, vanilla and walnuts.
3. Pour into a square dish and let cool. Cut into squares to serve.

Sauces And Dressings

Dressing

Vinaigrette

1 tbsp. Dijon mustard
1 tbsp. white wine vinegar
2 tbsp. olive oil
Salt and pepper to taste

Mix the mustard with the wine vinegar first. Then add the oil and mix well. Season with salt and pepper.

Strawberry Dressing

1 tbsp. Dijon mustard
1 tbsp. strawberry vinegar
2 tbsp. vegetable oil
1 strawberry, sliced

Mix the mustard and strawberry vinegar together.
Slowly add the oil.
Add sliced strawberry.

Lemon and Garlic Vinaigrette

1 tbsp. Dijon mustard
2 tbsp. lemon juice
3 tbsp. vegetable oil
1 garlic clove
Salt and pepper to taste

Mix the mustard and lemon juice together.
Slowly add the oil.
Season with salt and pepper
Add the full clove of garlic and let it rest for an hour.
Remove the garlic clove before serving.

Italian Dressing

2 tbsp. olive oil
2 tbsp. balsamic vinegar
1 tsp. oregano
1 tsp. parsley
1 tbsp. Parmesan
Salt and pepper to taste

Whisk together the olive oil, balsamic vinegar, oregano, parsley, Parmesan cheese, and salt and pepper.

Greek Dressing

6 tbsp. olive oil
1 tsp. dried oregano
1 lemon, juiced
Ground black pepper to taste

Whisk together the olive oil, oregano, lemon juice and black pepper. Pour dressing over salad, toss and serve.

Blue Cheese Dressing

½ cup mayonnaise
2 tbsp. thick cream
1 tbsp. white vinegar
1.8 oz blue cheese (Danish blue for example)
Salt and pepper to taste

Combine the cream, mayonnaise, and white vinegar in a small bowl. Crumble the blue cheese into the mixture and stir gently
Let it rest for 1 or 2 days.
Add salt and pepper to taste

Bacon dressing

2 slices bacon
2 tbsp. cider vinegar
1 tbsp. vegetable oil
2 tbsp. whole grain
mustard
Black pepper to taste

Cook bacon in a skillet and cut into thin strips.
Let it cool for few minutes and add the vinegar, mustard, salt and pepper, and oil, stirring at all time
Serve warm.

Mayonnaise

2 egg yolks
1 tbsp. Dijon mustard
2 tbsp. lemon juice
1 cup vegetable oil
Salt and pepper to taste

Place the 2 yolks in a mixing bowl. Add the mustard and lemon juice. Whisk for about 20 seconds.
Add the oil very slowly, whisking continuously.
Add salt and pepper to taste

Tartare Sauce

1/8 Spring onions, chopped
2 tbsp. capers, chopped
1 tbsp. fresh parsley
2 tbsp. tarragon
1 cup mayonnaise

Mix all ingredients together.

Red Wine Sauce

2 tbsp butter
½ onion
½ shallot
½ tbsp. all purpose flour
1 cup red wine
Salt and pepper to taste

Melt the butter and cook the onion and shallots until soft.
Add the flour.
Add the wine and cook for 5-10 minutes at medium heat.
Add salt and pepper to taste
This sauce is perfect for meat, such as beef or lamb.

Mushroom Sauce

3 tsp butter
1-garlic clove
¼ cup mushroom
(Portobello or shiitake)
sliced
1 tbsp. brandy
¼ cup beef stock
1 tbsp. whole grain
mustard
½ cup cream
Salt and black pepper to
taste

In a saucepan melt the butter and cook the garlic until soft.
Add mushrooms and cook for about 5 min
Add the brandy, beef stock, mustard, cream, and salt and pepper.
Cook another 5 minutes.

This sauce is excellent with meats and pasta.

Mustard Sauce

1 tbsp. whole grain
mustard
1 garlic clove
½ onion
2 tbsp. butter
½ cup white wine
Salt and pepper to taste

Melt the butter and cook the garlic and onion until soft.
Add mustard and white wine.
Add salt and pepper to taste
Cook for 10 minutes at medium heat.
This sauce is very good with veal, chicken, pork, or lamb

Honey and garlic marinade

2 tbsp olive oil
1 garlic chopped
1 lemon juice
2 tbsp honey
1 tbsp Thyme
1 cup of white wine
Salt and pepper to taste

In a large bowl, mix all ingredients together.
Marinade meat of fish for at least 1 hours

Chocolate Sauce

2 oz. semisweet chocolate
2 tbsp. dark rum
¼ cup light cream

Melt the chocolate with the rum and the cream in a bain marie (Pour the mixture into small ramekins and place the ramekins in a 9 x 13-inch baking pan. Add water to the pan until ramekins are sitting in 1 to 1 ½ inches of liquid. Don't let water get into the ramekins) and cook until the chocolate is completely melt
Serve with cake, ice cream….

Brandy Cream Sauce

2 egg yolks
1/3 cup caster (fine) sugar
1/3 cup brandy
1 cup Heavy cream
2 egg whites

In a small bowl, mix the egg yolks and sugar. Stir for few minutes
Add the brandy.
Add the whipped cream.
Stir well.
In a medium bowl, Beat egg whites with an electric mixer until stiff and add to the yolk mixture.

Crème Anglaise

4 egg yolks
4 tbsp granulated sugar
2 pint milk
2 vanilla beans

In a medium bowl mix the egg yolks and the sugar.
Boil the milk in a saucepan with the vanilla
Add the milk slowly to the yolk mixture and stir well.
Pour this into a saucepan and warm it up at medium heat until it becomes a bit thicker.
Let it cool.
Keep in the refrigerator for at least an hour before serving.

Strawberry Sauce

16 oz. frozen strawberries, thawed
2 tsp. cornstarch
1 tbsp. strawberry liquor

Thaw the strawberries.
In a small saucepan, combine juice from strawberries, liquor, and cornstarch.
Cook at medium heat for 2 to 3 minutes until the mixture thickens.
Add strawberries and cook for another 5 minutes over low heat.

Le

Menu

The following menus can be used to plan your 3 or 4-course meals using recipes from this book. Enjoy!

Moules Marinieres

Scallop in a White Wine Sauce Served with
Tagliatelle

Cheese Platter

Crème Brulee

Bruschetta

Veal Scaloppini Marsala with Garden Dish
Vegetable

Cheese Platter

White Chocolate Mousse

Goat Cheese Salad

Steak With a Blue Cheese Sauce With Garlic
Mash Potatoes

Mille-feuille With Apples, Calvados And Wild
Berries

Chinese Hot and Sour Soup

Duck With Pears and Raisin

Coconut flan with Caramel

Tabbouleh

Saffran Salmon Serve with Potatoes Pancake

Cheese Platter

Tarte Tatin with Vanilla Ice Cream

Entrepreneur/Mom

Is it possible to work minutes per day but make more money than if you worked a full time job? Is it possible to have unlimited cash flow without working at all? If you're interested in the answers to these questions I would like to recommend a book for you. The book is called ***Stop Working by Rohan Hall***. Stop Working teaches you how to build a business, and create unlimited cash flow with only minutes per day of your personal time. I think it's a book that moms and entrepreneurs alike will find valuable. It's time to stop working and start enjoying your life and your family.